A Note to Parents and Teachers

DK READERS is a compelling new reading programme for children, designed in conjunction with leading literacy experts, including Cliff Moon M.Ed., Honorary Fellow of the University of Reading. Cliff Moon has spent many years as a teacher and teacher educator specializing in reading and has written more than 140 books for children and teachers. He reviews regularly for teachers' journals.

Beautiful illustrations and superb full-colour photographs combine with engaging, easy-to-read stories to offer a fresh approach to each subject in the series. Each DK READER is guaranteed to capture a child's interest while developing his or her reading skills, general knowledge and love of reading.

The five levels of DK READERS are aimed at different reading abilities, enabling you to choose the books that are exactly right for each child:

Pre-level 1: Learning to read
Level 1: Beginning to read
Level 2: Beginning to read alone
Level 3: Reading alone
Level 4: Proficient readers

The "normal" age at which a child begins to read can be anywhere from three to eight years old, so these levels are intended only as a general guideline.

No matter which level you select, you can be sure that you are helping children learn to read, then read to learn!

LONDON, NEW YORK, MUNICH,
MELBOURNE, AND DELHI

Project Editor Penny Smith
Art Editor Susan Calver

Senior Editor Linda Esposito
Senior Art Editor Diane Thistlethwaite
Production Melanie Dowland
Picture Researcher Cynthia Frazer
Jacket Designer Dean Price
Indexer Lynn Bresler

Reading Consultant
Cliff Moon, M.Ed.

First published in Great Britain by
Dorling Kindersley Limited
80 Strand, London WC2 ORL
A Penguin Company

08 09 10 9 8 7 6 5 4 3

A CIP catalogue record for this book is
available from the British Library.

ISBN 978-0-7513-2842-4

Colour reproduction by Colourscan, Singapore
Printed and bound in China by L Rex Printing Co., Ltd.

The publisher would like to thank the following for their kind
permission to reproduce their photographs:
Key: t=top, a=above, b=below, l=left, r=right, c=centre,
Barnaby's Picture Library: Alistair Bruce 14br; **BBC Photograph
Library**: 13br; **J L Charmet**: 11tl; **Christie's Images**: 23a; **Corbis**: Lyn
Hughes 10bc; **Et archive**: 22br; **Image Bank**: 20a; **Barnabas
Kindersley**: 15bl, 15acr, 15bcr, 21cr; **Mary Evans Picture Library**: 28bl,
31tl; **Pictor International Ltd**: 8–9b; **Powerstock/Zefa**: 6ac, 28a;
Robert Harding Picture Library: A Autenzio/Explorer 29b; **Telegraph
Colour Library**: 19a; **Tony Stone Images**: Jerome Tisne 6br, 16–17b
All other images © Dorling Kindersley.
For further information see: www.dkimages.com

see our complete catalogue at

www.dk.com

DK READERS

BEGINNING TO READ ALONE

2

Holiday!

Celebration Days around the World

Written by Deborah Chancellor

DK

A Dorling Kindersley Book

Fun around the world

Throughout the year
people remember
special days.

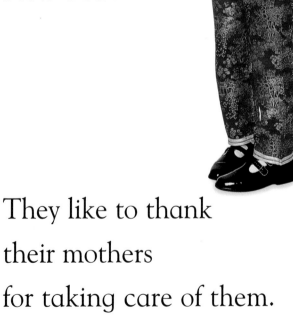

They like
to welcome in
the Chinese
New Year.

They like to thank
their mothers
for taking care of them.

They like
to dress up and
scare people
on Hallowe'en.

This book shows
special events
around the world.

And it tells us
what makes them
days to remember.

Chinese New Year

Between
January 21
and
February 20

The Chinese New Year

begins when there is

a new moon in the sky.

This means that it starts

on a different day each year.

Bouncing baby

The Chinese year 2000
is the year of the dragon.
Babies born in 2000
should be strong
and energetic!

Children dress up
in red silk clothes.
In China,
red stands
for happiness.

They are given
"lucky money"
in red and
gold envelopes.

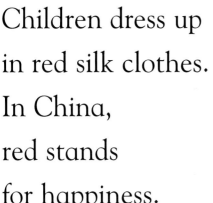

In cities around the world
there are parades in the streets.
Dragon dancers weave
in and out of the crowds.

They collect money and lettuce.
Lettuce is a symbol of new life.
The dragon stands for
long life and riches.

Valentine's Day

February 14

On Valentine's Day
people send gifts and cards.
These let others know
that someone loves them.

The story began
when a Roman emperor
banned men from marrying.
He wanted them
to join his army instead.

St Valentine
was a priest
who carried out
weddings in secret.
He was sentenced
to death.

On his last day he thanked
his jailer's daughter
for her friendship.
He signed his note,
"love from your Valentine".

Today, senders do not say
who the presents
and cards are from.

April Fool's Day

April
1

This is the day
when people play
tricks on each other.
April Fool's Day
began in France.

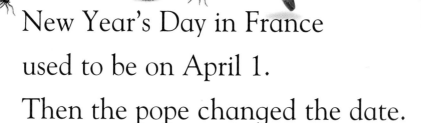

New Year's Day in France
used to be on April 1.
Then the pope changed the date.

Some people did not know and
kept using the old date.
They were laughed at and
called "April fools"

Sometimes, newspapers and
TV programmes trick people.

For example, spaghetti is made
from flour, eggs and water.
But one year a TV programme
showed spaghetti growing on trees!

Spaghetti

Mother's Day

Second Sunday in May

About 100 years ago
an American woman
named Anne Jarvis
asked her friends to wear
white carnations to church.

She wanted them to think
of her mother, who had died.

Mother's Day in Europe

American soldiers took
Mother's Day to Europe
during World War Two.
They sent gifts home
on Mother's Day.

In the UK, Mother's Day is held
in March or April, the time of
the old holiday of Mothering Sunday.

People give
their mothers
presents and cards.
Children help with
household jobs.

Father's Day

Third Sunday in June

An American,

Louise Smart Dodd,

was the first person

to celebrate Father's Day.

When her mother died,
her father had to bring up
six children on his own.

Roses are the flowers
for Father's Day.
Some people wear a red rose
if their father is alive
and a white rose
if he has died.

On Father's Day
people like to send
cards and presents.

Hallowe'en

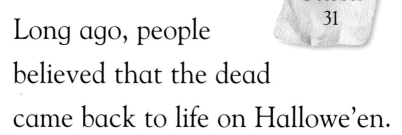

October
31

Long ago, people
believed that the dead
came back to life on Hallowe'en.

Today "Hallowe'en" means
the evening before All Saint's Day.
"Hallow" means "saint".

People remember Hallowe'en
by going to parties.
They dress up as ghosts
or scary skeletons.

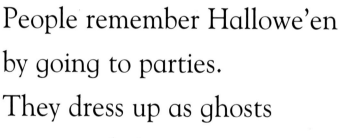

*Sweets are
often given
at Halloween.*

Apples ripen in the autumn
so they are used
in lots of Hallowe'en games.
Sometimes players bob for apples
in big buckets filled with water.

Pumpkin face

Some people make jack o' lanterns. These hollowed-out pumpkins are supposed to scare off the spooky spirits of the night!

Sometimes they bite at apples hung on string. The first person to bite an apple is said to be the first to marry the next year!

Diwali

Hindu is a religion in which people worship many gods. There are many Hindu writings about the adventures of these gods.

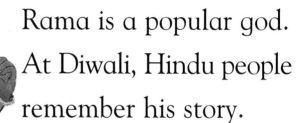

Rama

Rama is a popular god. At Diwali, Hindu people remember his story.

Rama was once driven from his kingdom by a wicked demon. The demon kidnapped Rama's wife, Sita.

Rama and his wife Sita

Rama fought a fierce battle.
He won back his wife and
returned to his kingdom in triumph.

The elephant god
Ganesh is another Hindu god.
Ganesh's father cut off
his son's head by mistake.
He put an elephant's head
in its place.

People decorate their houses
with twinkling lights
called divas.
These lights
are meant
to guide
Rama home.

They also
decorate floors
in their houses
with patterns
called rangoli.
These are to
welcome visitors.

People give each other
cards and sweets at Diwali.

Christmas

December 25

Long, long ago
Jesus Christ was born in a stable.
Christians around the world
mark this event with Christmas.

Children put on nativity plays
to tell the story of the birth.

People give each other
presents and cards.

Families decorate
fir trees at Christmas.
These evergreens
are a symbol of
everlasting life.

Many children believe
Santa Claus brings presents
the night before Christmas.
He is said to ride on a sleigh
pulled by reindeer.

The first Santa Claus

"Santa Claus" comes from
the Dutch word for St Nicholas.
This saint was a rich bishop
who used his wealth
to help poor people.

He climbs down chimneys and
fills stockings with presents
for children.

Kwanzaa

This means "first fruits".

At Kwanzaa, African Americans celebrate the African harvest.

Plantain　　　　*Okra*　　　　*Cassava*

They think of their dead relatives who lived in Africa as well as the African way of life.

Aseye lives in Africa

Forced to America

Africans were taken
to America as slaves.
They were put in chains
and packed onto
crowded slave ships.

Sweetcorn

Yam

Sweet potato

Kwanzaa lasts
seven days.
Each day people
light candles.
Families feast
and give presents.

Tim lives in America

More days to remember

Every year a spectacular carnival
takes place in Rio de Janeiro, Brazil.
Samba schools join a huge parade.
They show off new dances and costumes.

St Patrick's Day celebrates the life
of the patron saint of Ireland.
In some cities green beer is served and
rivers are even dyed green!

In Japan, Hina Matsuri
is a day dedicated to dolls.
Dolls take away bad luck
when they are cast out to sea.

At the Indian festival of Holi
people cover each other
with bright powder paint.
This celebrates the god Krishna
and how he soaked
his companion Rada
with coloured water.

People think about new life at Easter.
Chocolate eggs are popular –
in Australia an enormous egg
weighed as much as ten horses!

Hanukkah is the Festival of Lights.
It is when Jewish people remember
how the Temple of Jerusalem was cleansed.
A candle is lit each night at Hanukkah.